# INVENTIONS!

# INVENTIONS!

## MOIRA BUTTERFIELD

W
FRANKLIN WATTS
LONDON · SYDNEY

## Weird True Facts! the boring stuff...

This edition published 2014 by Franklin Watts

Copyright © Franklin Watts 2014
Franklin Watts
338 Euston Road
London NW1 3BH

Franklin Watts Australia
Level 17/207 Kent Street
Sydney, NSW 2000

A CIP catalogue record for this book is available from the British Library.

Dewey no: 600

ISBN: 978 1 4451 2968 6

Printed in China.

Franklin Watts is a division of Hachette Children's Books, an Hachette UK company

www.hachette.co.uk

Series editor: Sarah Ridley
Editor in Chief: John C. Miles
Designer: www.rawshock.co.uk/Jason Anscomb
Art director: Jonathan Hair
Picture research: Diana Morris

# CONTENTS

## BRILLIANT BACK THEN!

Early inventions helped humans to evolve from cave-dwelling hunters to sophisticated house-dwellers. In fact, some of the world's first inventions proved so helpful we still use them today.

## ANCIENT INVENTIONS TIMELINE

**2.9 million–2 million years** BCE
Early humans invented the first ever tools, made from pieces of stone, for hunting and cutting up meat.

**40,000–8000** BCE
Humans invented pottery, cave painting and carving. The first carved statuettes were made, showing small fat female figures.

**8000–5000** BCE
Crops were first harvested, and grinding stones were invented to grind up the grain for cooking. Weaving looms and ways of making copper objects were all invented, too.

**2000–500** BCE
All kinds of new inventions arrived, including the first ever machines using gears, weapons such as giant catapults, and instruments to help sailors navigate by the Sun, Moon and stars.

**4000–3000** BCE
The first written language was invented, in Uruk (now in modern Iraq). It was made up of pictures, not letters. Other inventions around this time included bronze objects and the first ever wheels.

**500** BCE–**1** CE
Inventions that appeared in the ancient Roman Empire included aqueducts, fast-drying cement, underfloor central heating, apartment blocks, cross-bladed scissors and the letter G.

## Out East

Tea, the compass, paper, silk, the waterproof umbrella, the kite and the wheelbarrow all came from ancient China. Legend has it that silk was invented in 2700 BCE when a silkworm cocoon dropped from a tree into the teacup of Empress Si-Ling-Chi. The cocoon's strong silky threads unravelled and she got the credit for deciding to weave them into fabric.

**Modern equipment for extracting threads from silkworm cocoons. Soaking them in water aids the process.**

## GOD-LIKE GENIUS

In ancient Roman times clever inventors used science to create illusions that people thought were the work of the gods. The Temple of Serapis in Alexandria had an iron chariot floating magically near the ceiling, perhaps secretly held there by magnets. Hero of Alexandria built the world's first automatic opening doors in a temple and designed statues that appeared to talk.

## World's first computer?

In 1900 the world's oldest known calculating machine was recovered from an ancient Roman shipwreck. It is called the Antikythera Mechanism (see right), after the island near where it was found. It was built around 100 BCE, and had internal wheels and cogs that could make complex mathematical calculations on the position of the stars, Moon and Sun. It also recorded the year when the next ancient Olympic Games was going to be held.

**A reconstruction of the bronze Antikythera Mechanism. Fragments recovered from the shipwreck were used to work out what it looked like.**

## IT'LL NEVER WORK!

In the years between 1000 and 1500 CE there were lots of surprising inventions. Some we only know about from pictures in early books and documents.

Leonardo's parachute – a triangular-shaped wooden frame covered in linen. Nobody actually tried using a parachute of any kind until the late 1700s.

### He got there first

Artist and inventor Leonardo Da Vinci (1452-1519 CE) lived in Italy and France during the Renaissance, a time when there were many new developments in art and science. When he wasn't painting masterpieces such as the *Mona Lisa*, he was sketching ideas for new inventions far ahead of their time, such as helicopters, tanks, submarines and robots. Although Leonardo never built any of these to our knowledge, modern engineers have tried reconstructing them from his sketches and notes. The parachute, shown left, worked well.

A medieval picture of an alchemist experimenting, using magical spells as well as science.

## SCIENCE IS MAGIC

Medieval alchemists believed that they could turn ordinary materials such as lead into gold, and create an eternal life potion. They mixed up their science with magic, believing they had to use magical spells and symbols to make their experiments successful. They never succeeded, but whilst trying, they did invent lots of useful chemical equipment.

## FOUND IN FIGHT BOOKS

European medieval 'fight books' were catalogues of weaponry and fighting skills compiled by 'fight masters' – war experts that could be hired to train soldiers. Surviving copies show lots of war-like invention ideas, including weird battle weapons and even a diving suit.

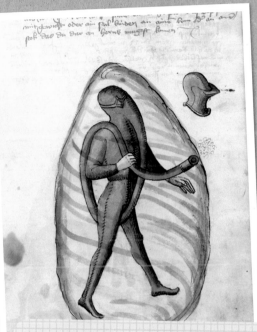

This leather diving suit design was sketched in a medieval fight book by Hans Talhoffer. When reconstructed, it worked well.

## Before and after

Medieval times also saw the invention of...

- **Glasses** Before this, people just suffered bad eyesight, though Seneca, an ancient Roman writer, is said to have looked through water-filled globes to read books.

- **Armour and gunpowder** Before gunpowder people fought with swords, and before armour they wore protective clothing made of leather.

- **The toothbrush** Before this, people cleaned their teeth using sticks.

- **Clocks** Before this, people told the time using hour glasses or sundials.

- **Horse stirrups and horseshoes** Before this, riders had to hold on tightly with their knees.

- **Buttonholes** Before this, buttons were just used as decoration.

- **The printing press** Before this, books were copied out by hand.

Sixteenth-century armour

## MARCH OF THE MACHINES

In the 1700s and 1800s European and American engineers and scientists made discoveries that completely changed the way people worked and lived. This period in history is called the Industrial Revolution.

### HALL OF FAME

Some of the most important inventors of the Industrial Revolution:

**James Hargreaves**

**Born:** Oswaldtwistle, England, 1720

**Invention:** The Spinning Jenny in 1769, a machine that could spin cotton much more quickly than people spinning by hand.

**Amazing fact:** Hargreaves never went to school and was never taught to read or write.

**Joseph Priestley**

**Born:** Birstall Fieldhead, England, 1733

**Invention:** Scientist who discovered a number of gases, including oxygen.

**Amazing fact:** Also invented the pencil rubber.

**James Watt**

**Born:** Greenock, Scotland, 1736

**Invention:** The first efficient and practical working steam engine.

**Amazing fact:** His aunt said: "I never saw such an idle boy," after she saw him spend half an hour taking the lid off a kettle and putting it back on again.

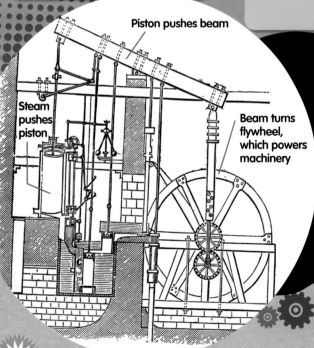

Piston pushes beam

Steam pushes piston

Beam turns flywheel, which powers machinery

### Full steam ahead

Steam was the driving force of the Industrial Revolution. A steam engine (left) works when burning coal heats up water inside a boiler. The water turns into steam and expands, pushing pistons that power machinery parts as they move back and forth.

## SHARING OR STEALING?

Britain tried to keep its new textile machine inventions secret. No machine parts, machine designs or textile workers were allowed out of the country. But young textile expert Samuel Slater disguised himself as a farmer and sneaked over to the USA to make a new life, and took the secrets of the new machinery with him. He founded the American spinning industry.

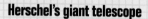

Herschel's giant telescope

**Eli Whitney**

**Born:** Massachusetts, USA, 1765

**Invention:** The cotton gin, to separate cotton seeds and fibre mechanically.

**Amazing fact:** He made no money from his cotton gin invention because everyone else copied it without paying him.

**William Herschel**

**Born:** Hanover, Germany, 1738

**Invention:** Built a powerful telescope and discovered Uranus, the first planet identified in modern times.

**Amazing fact:** He was once a musician in a regimental band.

**Edmund Cartwright**

**Born:** Nottingham, England, 1743

**Invention:** The first weaving machine, a steam-driven loom.

**Amazing fact:** He went bankrupt, and many of his machines were smashed up by angry workers fearful of losing their jobs.

Whitney's cotton gin

## INVENTIONS UNHAPPINESS

The machines of the Industrial Revolution brought unemployment to many because they carried out work once done by hand. Angry English textile workers, nicknamed 'Luddites', smashed up some of the weaving machines, and farm workers rioted, too. Many of the rioters were hanged or transported – banished to tough foreign prison colonies such as Australia.

Angry workers smashing weaving machinery.

## IF YOU DARE!

**If you're feeling off-colour today you might not want to read about these crazy, scary or downright weird medical inventions!**

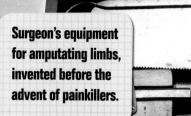

Surgeon's equipment for amputating limbs, invented before the advent of painkillers.

### That hurt...

The earliest known surgical procedure is trephining (also called trepanning), which means cutting a small hole in the skull. Stone Age skulls have been found with trephining holes, cut using stone tools. The ancient Egyptians made skull holes, supposedly to cure migraines, then used the skull scrapings to make potions.

In medieval times barbers did surgery alongside their normal job of cutting hair. They had tools such as knives and hooks, but the only pain-relief was alcohol or dangerous herbal potions made from poisons such as hemlock. By the early 1800s new fearsomely-sharp amputation knives had been designed to make surgery quicker, but it wasn't until 1846 that anaesthetic pain relief was finally invented.

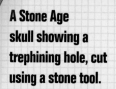

A Stone Age skull showing a trephining hole, cut using a stone tool.

### GERM ZAPPER

British surgeon Joseph Lister was the first person to realise that germs could infect wounds. He invented a hand pump that sprayed out carbolic acid during surgery, to kill germs. The acid covered everyone and everything in the operating room and it did kill germs but, unknown to Lister, it was also dangerous to breathe in.

Lister's 'donkey engine', a hand pump for spraying out acid during surgery, in use.

Etruscan false teeth (left), first designed nearly 3,000 years ago.

# SOME SURGICAL SURPRISES

The first people to invent false teeth were the Etruscans, who lived in Italy around 700 BCE. They made teeth from bone, ivory or cattle teeth, fixed in the mouth with gold bands.

US President George Washington (top right) famously had false teeth. He owned sets made from cow teeth, human teeth and even hippopotamus ivory. But, contrary to legend, he did not have any sets of wooden teeth.

The earliest known prosthetics (false body parts) are artificial toes, found fitted to two ancient Egyptian mummies. One of the toes was made from wood and leather, and the other from papier-mache.

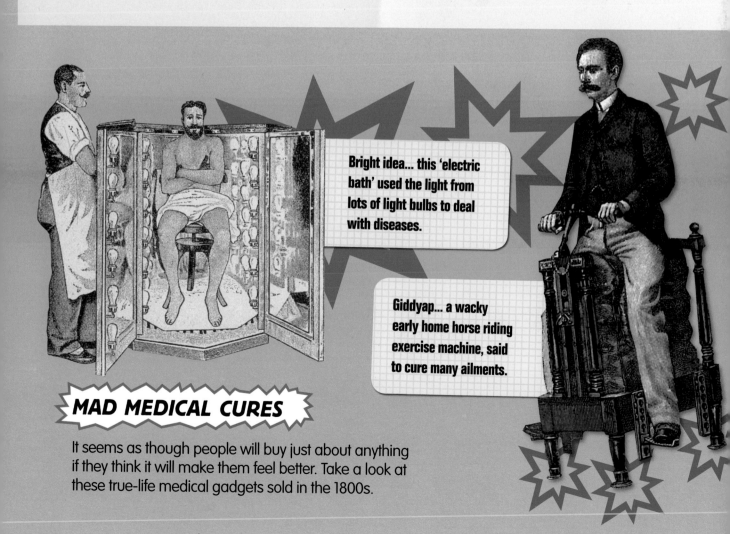

Bright idea... this 'electric bath' used the light from lots of light bulbs to deal with diseases.

Giddyap... a wacky early home horse riding exercise machine, said to cure many ailments.

# MAD MEDICAL CURES

It seems as though people will buy just about anything if they think it will make them feel better. Take a look at these true-life medical gadgets sold in the 1800s.

## TRAINS, PLANES AND BIRDMEN

For centuries inventors have tried to make transport vehicles of all kinds. Some have had more success than others...

### TRANSPORT TIMELINE

**3500 BCE**
The first carts and chariots with wheels appear.

**3000-2000 BCE**
World's first wooden boats built.

**1500s CE**
Noblemen started riding in horse-drawn carriages.

**1620**
First submarine built and tested.

**1740**
First powered motor carriage, run using clockwork.

**1783**
First practical steamboat demonstrated.

**1783**
The first passenger-carrying hot air balloon flight.

**1801**
First prototype steam-powered railway locomotive, built by Englishman Richard Trevithick.

**1814**
George Stephenson built the first practical steam-powered railway locomotive. The first railway opened in 1825.

**1853**
The first successful heavier-than-air aircraft (a glider) takes flight.

**1861**
First pedal-powered bicycle.

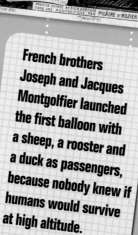

French brothers Joseph and Jacques Montgolfier launched the first balloon with a sheep, a rooster and a duck as passengers, because nobody knew if humans would survive at high altitude.

Richard Trevithick built this 'Catch Me Who Can' early steam ride in Euston Square, London, in 1808.

Over the centuries many people have tried to invent human-powered flying contraptions without success, plunging to Earth as they flapped their homemade wings.

In 1507, Italian John Damian tried to impress the Scottish king James IV by jumping off Stirling Castle wearing feathered wings. He fell into a dung heap and broke his leg.

Italian clockmaker Denis Bolin designed wings that flapped with a spring mechanism, but plunged to his death from the top of a French cathedral in 1536.

Eilmer, the flying monk, jumped off the tower of Malmesbury Abbey in England sometime before 1100 CE, wearing wings made from willow and cloth. He glided for 200m before crashing and breaking both legs. His abbot banned him from ever flying again.

Russian cosmonaut, Yuri Gagarin, the first human to travel into space, in 1961.

## WOULD YOU LIKE ONE OF THESE?

These up-to-date transport inventions might prove popular. What do you think?

The Martin Jetpack can soar up to nearly 2500m (8,000ft). It can travel 50km (31 miles) and has a handy parachute. If you'd like one, you'll need to pay $100,000.

The AIRpod car doesn't need fuel. It's powered by compressed air, and it might one day replace small vehicles such as golf carts.

The Martin Jetpack, with rotors on either side of a 2-stroke engine.

**1961**
World's first manned space flight.

**1903**
World's first successful powered aeroplane flight.

**1900**
World's first successfully-flown airship.

**1885**
First petrol-powered car.

The Wright brothers achieved the first powered aeroplane flight at Kitty Hawk, North Carolina, USA.

## AROUND THE HOUSE

Life at home has been hugely improved by inventors coming up with new ways to make it more convenient.

### Top five handy home helps

**1. Suck it up** In 1901, British engineer Herbert Cecil Booth invented the first electric vacuum machine. It was called the Puffing Billy, and the well-to-do could hire it to visit their home. It was so big it sat on a horse-drawn cart attached to a 30m-long hose.

**2. Cool invention** In 1876 German Carl von Linde worked out how to liquify gas, the process used to keep fridges cool, though the first fridges were so large they had to have their own room.

**3. Lush flush** King Minos of Crete had a flushing toilet as far back as 1700 BCE, but flushing loos as we know them didn't appear until the end of the 1700s, and then only in the wealthiest homes. Before that time, people used chamber pots which they had to empty by hand, throwing the contents into the street or into a hole in the ground.

**4. Wooden wipe** Toilet paper was first made in ancient China for the exclusive use of Chinese emperors. The first modern-style paper appeared in the late 1800s, though early versions were rough and sometimes contained wood splinters.

**5. Melting man** In 1946 US scientist Percy L. Spencer was standing next to a magnetron power tube, part of some radar equipment, when he felt a chocolate bar melting in his pocket. His discovery led him to invent the microwave oven, though the first ones were huge, at around 1.6m (5.2ft) tall.

The first 'fridgedaire', made by the Delco Light company in the USA.

This vacuum cleaner of the early 1900s was absolutely enormous!!

The first microwave ovens were enormous and looked extremely dangerous.

This early bread slicer looks more like something a plumber would use to cut pipes.

# HISTORIC HOME SURPRISES

**The host with the most** Ancient Roman Emperor Nero impressed guests with a giant revolving dining room at his Golden Palace in Rome. Archaeologists have found the remains, mounted on revolving spheres hidden under the floor. Above the slowly turning room, ceiling panels slid back to shower the diners with perfume or flower petals.

**Shocking prongs** Forks were first used in the Far East but only arrived in Europe in the 1200s, when a Venetian noblewoman was seen using a small gold one in public. The Catholic Church considered the new-fangled fork a wicked invention, and forks didn't come into common use until the 1700s.

**China spy** The Chinese invented porcelain china by mixing clay with minerals, and they kept their method a secret until French priest Francois Xavier D'Entrecolles discovered how they did it. He sent their secrets home to Europe, where manufacturers quickly copied them.

## Kitchen creations

**Has anyone brought a hammer?** The first tin cans were invented in 1810, but they could only be opened with a hammer. Luckily, can-openers were invented in 1858.

**Sliced bread becomes best** US inventor Otto Frederick Rohwedder invented a machine to slice and wrap loaves in 1928. Handily, the pop-up toaster was invented around the same time.

**Millionaire morning person** US businessman Will Keith Kellogg invented cornflakes – the first breakfast cereal – in 1906. He gave away free samples and put prizes inside cereal boxes for the first time, so he invented the free promotional giveaway, too. He soon became a multimillionaire.

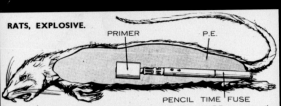

# SECRET STUFF

Spies need special inventions such as hidden cameras and weapons. Here is some real-life secret spy kit.

## COLD WAR KIT

In the decades after World War Two, western democratic countries and eastern communist countries did not actually go to war but they had a tense stand-off, called the Cold War. Here is some of the amazing spy equipment used during that time.

**Covert cameras** The CIA (the US Central Intelligence Agency) invented lots of Cold War spying gadgets. These included a camera disguised as a tiny dragonfly and a camera that could be attached to pigeons.

**Fake fashion** An evening outfit was designed for a CIA woman spy, with mini cameras and recording devices hidden in the accessories.

**Dung devices** CIA aircraft pilots could be directed to secret sites by a homing beacon hidden inside a fake animal poo.

**Log listener** This reconstruction (below) shows a bug hidden inside a fake tree stump. The real one was placed in a Moscow wood by the CIA to intercept signals from a Soviet air base.

---

### RATS, EXPLOSIVE.

PRIMER    P.E.

PENCIL TIME FUSE

A rat is skinned, the skin being sewn up and filled with P.E. to assume the shape of a dead rat. A Standard No. 6 Primer is set in the P.E. Initiation is by means of a short length of safety fuse with a No. 27 detonator crimped on one end, and a copper tube igniter on the other end, or, as in the case of the illustration above, a P.T.F. with a No. 27 detonator attached. The rat is then left amongst the coal beside a boiler and the flames initiate the safety fuze when the rat is thrown on to the fire, or as in the case of the P.T.F. a Time Delay is used.

## World War Two specials

During World War Two the SOE (Special Operations Executive) was set up by the British to sabotage enemy forces. Its agents were trained to kill with their bare hands, disguise themselves and use an array of special equipment.

SOE inventions included magnetised trouser buttons. When cut off the trousers and put on top of each other, they worked as a compass. Other devices included dead rats filled with explosives (above), a fold-up motorbike and land mines disguised as dollops of animal poo.

This tiny CIA camera was disguised as a dragonfly.

A solar-powered bug hidden inside a fake log. It intercepted Soviet air base signals and sent them to a US satellite.

**Shoe signals** The Romanian Secret Service waited for foreign diplomats to order new shoes, then intercepted the shoe delivery and hid bugs in the shoe heels. The bug then went wherever the diplomat went!

**Loaded lippy** The Soviet KGB gave its female spies a tiny one-shot pistol disguised as a lipstick.

A Romanian spy bug hidden inside the heel of a shoe.

This KGB-designed lipstick pistol was capable of one shot.

## A MURDEROUS MOMENT

Secret agents try to keep their gadgets secret, but one deadly invention came to light in 1978 in a shocking way, when writer and broadcaster Georgi Markov was killed, most likely by the Bulgarian Secret Service. Walking along a London street, he felt a jab in his thigh and turned to see a man pick up an umbrella and get into a taxi. Four days later Markov died, the victim of a poison-tipped umbrella point that had left a deadly pellet in his body.

An umbrella similar to the one used on Georgi Markov, adapted to deliver a pin-head sized pellet of deadly poison.

## IMPOSSIBLE OR COMING SOON?

In the world of science-fiction – imaginary stories of space travel and the future – all kinds of exciting inventions have been dreamt up. But are they possible in real life?

X-ray specs, a popular toy that fakes the impression of looking at an X-ray.

This airport body scanner creates a picture of the body using reflected radio waves.

### HOW TO SEE THROUGH THINGS

X-ray specs were once sold as an incredible way to see through to people's bones, but in reality they were fake toys. However, if you go on an airline you might encounter a real-life machine that can see body shapes through clothes. Airport body scanners send radio waves towards the body, and the machine measures the way the radio waves reflect back, to create a picture of the body and detect any hidden objects.

Scientists have been trying to create a way to see through ordinary material. They have been working with atoms (the tiny building blocks that make up all objects), getting them to interact with a laser beam to turn them transparent. This seems to work on a very tiny scale, so perhaps one day someone will really invent a way to see through walls!

The built-in strength of an exoskeleton suit means a soldier could do unlimited press-ups!

### How to be a superhero

In the Iron Man movies the hero has a robot suit that makes him into a superhero with incredible strength. Although not in the superhero league, a soldier might soon be able to triple his strength by wearing an exoskeleton – a robot suit with hydraulically-powered arms and legs. These suits are now being tested by the military, and might soon be used for lifting heavy battle equipment.

## HOW TO GET TELEPORTED

In *Star Trek*, space travellers can be 'beamed' from one location to another – turned into particles that are sent instantly somewhere else and then turned back into a human. The computer power needed to do this is way beyond current science, even if such a process was possible, which it isn't for large objects such as humans.

However, a type of teleporting is possible in the very tiny world of quantum particles – the miniscule particles inside an atom. Scientists have been able to teleport energy between tiny particles of light called photons, and they hope to use the science to teleport information, though not people or objects.

An artist's impression of a wormhole in space, that could connect different times.

### How to time-travel

Nobody has time-travelled yet, as far as we know, but scientists have come up with several theories of how it could be possible. One way to do it might be to find a 'wormhole', a tunnel shape in space that allows you to travel between two different times. Nobody has ever proved that wormholes exist, but in theory they could.

CLASSICS Illustrated
Featuring Stories by the World's Greatest Authors
No. 133  15¢

THE TIME MACHINE
H. G. WELLS

A time machine as imagined in the 1960s.

## THANKS FOR THESE!

Here are some inventions that have proved very popular with children.

### PLAYTIME GENIUS

**Pharaoh's fun** The ancient Egyptians invented the first known board game, called 'Senet', found in tombs dating to 3100 BCE. Pieces were moved around squares on a Senet board, but nobody knows the exact rules. The ancient Egyptians also had stone marbles and wooden dolls to play with.

**Get reading** In 1658 a Czech teacher called Amos Komensky published the world's first picture book for children, an encyclopedia called the *Orbis Pictus*. It had a whopping 150 chapters, illustrated with woodcuts.

**Yo-yos get going** Yo-yo-type toys have been around for centuries but they got their modern name from the Philippines, where yo-yos with sharp edges were once used as weapons. Yo-yo is a Philippino word meaning 'come back'.

**Inventor dudes** In the 1950s Californian surfers put rollerskate wheels on their boards and invented the skateboard. Several people seem to have come up with the idea at the same time.

The ever-popular skateboard was invented in the 1950s.

# Yummy stuff

**Bubbling up** The ancient Greeks and the Mayans chewed tree resin, but modern chewing gum was first invented by US brothers Henry and Frank Fleer in 1880. They sold small pieces coated with sugar. The first bubble gum, called 'double bubble', was invented in 1928 and the entire first batch sold out in one afternoon.

**Cool creation** Forms of fruity, creamy, iced dessert were eaten in the Middle East and China before the fashion spread, but it was the early American colonists who first called it 'ice cream'. US President George Washington loved it and spent $200 on it in the summer of 1790, a fortune in those days.

**Chocolate bar breakthrough** The world's first chocolate bar was invented in 1847 by Englishman Joseph Fry, though the first bar was much rougher and more bitter-tasting than today's versions.

A nineteenth-century ice cream vendor with a crowd of eager customers.

A 'baby cage' in use outside a New York apartment block.

# Maybe not...

**Don't look down, baby!** In 1937 the 'baby cage' was invented, to give city-dwelling babies fresh air. The cage was designed to hang outside the windows of high buildings.

## WHEN IT ALL WENT WRONG

Inventing can be a risky business leading to accidents, as these sometimes tragic true stories prove.

A statue of Galileo Galilei.

GALILEO GALILEI

A cartoon of Humphrey Davy looking as if he has sniffed too many chemicals.

### THE FAMOUS FAIL

Even the world's most successful inventors can have their off-moments…

**Stop sun-staring** Italian genius Galileo Galilei, born in 1564, achieved so much in science that he is often called 'the Father of Physics'. But he spent so many hours studying the Sun that he very nearly went blind.

**Davy, don't!** British chemist Sir Humphrey Davy discovered several important chemicals in the 1700s, but had a habit of sniffing the chemicals he worked with, which nearly killed him.

**Edison, Oops!** As a young man, famous nineteenth-century US inventor Thomas Edison was fired from a newspaper job because he secretly experimented with chemicals while on the nightshift and spilt acid on the floor. It dripped down onto the boss's desk below.

Henry Winstanley's doomed Eddystone Lighthouse.

## Inventors meet their end

Some inventors paid for their work with their lives.

**Fallen man** English engineer Henry Winstanley wanted to experience a heavy storm at the Eddystone Lighthouse, built to his design on rocks in the sea near Plymouth, England. In 1703 he did just that, and died when it collapsed around him.

**Parachute plunge** Franz Reichelt, an Austrian tailor, confidently jumped off the Eiffel Tower in 1912, wearing his self-designed parachute jacket. Sadly he plunged to his death in front of the invited crowd.

**Tragic taster** Brilliant Swedish-German chemist Karl Scheele discovered many chemical elements but made the mistake of tasting his new discoveries. He died of mercury-poisoning in 1786.

**Deadly discovery** Polish-French scientist Marie Curie discovered radioactivity. Sadly she did not realise how dangerous radioactive material was, and often carried it round in her pocket or kept it in her desk drawer, liking its pretty green glow. She died in 1934 of cancer caused by radiation.

**Kitchen creator** Nineteenth-century German chemist Christian Schonbein waited until his wife was away, then cooked up some acids in the kitchen. He spilt the mixture and mopped it up with her apron, only to find that it burst into flames! He had accidentally invented a chemical mixture called guncotton, which was then used in firearms and for making the first photographic film.

Marie Curie won the Nobel Prize twice for her scientific discoveries.

Charles Goodyear's invention — 'vulcanised' rubber — helped drive the motor vehicle industry forward.

## ACCIDENTAL INVENTING

Sometimes inventing accidents can lead to triumphs.

**Chemical cook-up** American inventor Charles Goodyear is said to have invented tyre rubber in 1839 by accidentally dropping some rubber mixed with chemicals onto a stove.

**Sweet success** German chemist Constantine Hahlberg accidentally invented the sweetener saccharine when he spilt chemicals on his hands and forgot to wash them before eating lunch. He noticed that the mixture on his hands made his lunch taste unusually sweet.

# PLUGGED-IN PEOPLE

## ELECTRONIC PIONEERS

Nowadays TVs, computers and mobile phones are ordinary objects, but who came up with the ideas first?

An early Bell telephone, built in 1877.

## PLUG-IN PIONEERS

**Is that you, Mr Edison?** Thomas Edison invented the phonograph, the first machine that could record and play sound. The first sentence he recorded and played back was "Mary had a little lamb".

**Bell rings** The credit for the first practical working telephone goes to US inventor Alexander Graham Bell. He made the first successful two-way phone call, talking to his assistant in another room in his house. The first ever words he spoke into a phone were: "Watson, come here! I want to see you!"

**TV times** Scotsman John Logie Baird was the first person to successfully transmit a TV picture in public, in 1926. He sent a picture of a ventriloquist's dummy called 'Snooky Bill' between two rooms, via what he called his 'Televisor'.

**Mobile men** Two US engineers – Joel Engel and Richard Frenkiel – worked out the basics of modern mobile technology in the early 1970s. The first phones were as big as bricks and cost up to £3,000.

A giant early mobile phone next to a more modern version.

An early computer, dating from the 1950s. It was so big it filled a whole room.

# COMPUTER CREATIONS

**Big and little** The first computers were so huge they took up whole rooms. They were developed in the 1940s and 50s, though people argue over which was the first. The first laptop computer was the Osborne 1, which appeared in 1981. It had a tiny little screen measuring 12.5cm (5in) across.

**Game on** People argue over what was the first ever computer game, but the first popular video game was a table tennis game called Pong, invented in the USA by Nolan Bushnell. In Pong a blip bounced back and forth between two lines that represented ping-pong bats.

**Starting small** Steve Jobs and Steve Wozniak sold their prized possessions to set up Apple Computers in 1976, and they eventually changed the way that computers and mobile phones looked and worked. Jobs sold his VW van and Wozniak sold his computerised calculator to start up their business in the Jobs family garage.

Pong, the latest in home entertainment in 1975. You plugged the game into the TV.

Steve Jobs, founder of Apple Computers. His company has had a huge effect on computer design.

Here are some new developments that might lead to the world changing in your lifetime!

## Mind-reading machinery

Scientists are working on mapping the brain and recording the brainwaves created by everyday actions such as seeing, hearing or moving. These can be detected and used to control machines. Japanese company Toyota has designed a wheelchair that can be moved by mind signals picked up through a helmet that measures brain activity. They've also created a cycle helmet that allows cyclists to change gear using mindpower.

In the future it's predicted that entire brains will be scanned and simulated on super-powerful computers. You might even be able to log on to see your own brain simulation and ask the computer to work out why you have a headache or feel unhappy.

## FEEL THE FORCE

It's possible that a spaceship will travel to Mars and a permanent base could be built on the Moon. But astronauts face the danger of radiation from the Sun, which is much stronger above Earth's atmosphere and can lead to serious illness. NASA scientists are investigating ways to protect space-travellers. One idea is to have portable fabric balloons that can be plugged in to create an electric radiation-repelling force field around a moonbase or a space buggy.

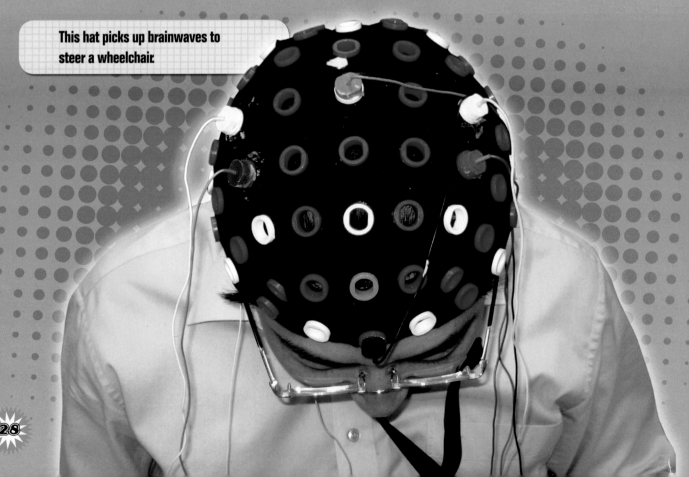

This hat picks up brainwaves to steer a wheelchair.

Genetic medicine may one day allow humans to have many more birthdays.

## Life-lengthening pills

Scientists are busy looking at the reasons why body cells get old, in order to invent life-prolonging medicines. Your genes, the instructions found in every cell inside your body, might hold the key to living longer, and scientists may be able to switch genes on or off to ensure you reach some very big birthdays!

# FEELING ROBOTS

Robots may soon be able to feel objects in the same way that we do. US scientists have created a type of robot skin made of a thin layer of tiny particles. They squeeze together and send out tiny light signals when they touch something, and the light signals can be measured to create a picture of what the skin is touching.

It's likely that robot parts will increasingly be placed inside people's bodies. One cybernetics (robot) expert even put a microchip inside his arm, so he could automatically open doors without touching the doorhandle!

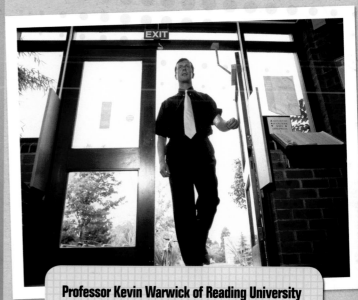

Professor Kevin Warwick of Reading University opens a door with his microchipped arm.

# FUTURE LIST

Here are some more futuristic science predictions that could be on the way to reality.

• Body-sensitive clothing that detects how you feel and warns you when you are ill.

• Shuttle-style space planes that zip around the world above the Earth's atmosphere.

• Artificial trees created to suck up pollution from the air.

• Cheap petrol created by bacteria instead of being brought up from oil wells.

• Replicator copiers – 3D scanners that can recreate a 3D object from a scan, using metal and plastic. These already exist, but perhaps they will turn up in everyone's homes.

**Airship** A craft filled with lighter-than-air gas and fitted with motors to propel it through the air.

**Alchemy** The idea that ordinary metals could be turned into gold. Medieval inventors tried lots of ways to do this, but never succeeded.

**Amputation** Cutting off a limb. Before anaesthetics were invented this often had to be done without painkillers.

**Antikythera Mechanism** The world's first known calculating machine, dating from around 100 BCE.

**Atom** A tiny particle of something. Everything is made up of atoms.

**Automata** A mechanical robot that works using cogs and wheels.

**Bronze Age** Roughly 3300 to 1000 BCE, a time when humans worked out how to use copper and bronze to make objects.

**Chemical** A substance that can't be separated out into any other substances.

**CIA** The Central Intelligence Agency, the US government spy organisation.

**Cold War** A period between 1945 and 1991, when democratic countries and Communist countries were hostile to each other.

**Cotton gin** A machine invented in 1765 for separating out cotton seeds and fibres.

**Cybernetics** The science of robots.

**Electronic** Powered by tiny particles called electrons, moving as an electric current.

**Exoskeleton** A skeleton shape worn on the outside of the body.

**Fight book** A medieval fighting manual, often showing pictures of unusual medieval machines.

**Force field** An invisible wall of energy particles.

**Germs** Tiny organisms that are harmful to human health.

**Hot air balloon** A giant balloon that can float when the air inside it is heated up.

**Industrial Revolution** A period in the 1700s and 1800s when scientists and engineers made lots of discoveries that completely changed the way people lived and worked.

**Iron Age** Roughly 1000 BCE to 400 CE, a time when humans learnt how to make objects from iron.

**Jetpack** A jet-powered backpack that enables people to fly.

**Laser** A device that emits a beam of light that can be aimed.

**Locomotive** A powered vehicle that pulls or pushes trucks along a railway line.

**Luddites** Angry English workers who rioted during the 1700s, in protest at machines taking their jobs.

**Mass-production** When an object is made over and over again, identically, by machine.

**Mechanics** Harnessing the power of objects when they are made to move, using such equipment as wheels and gears.

**Molecule** A small particle of something, made up of even smaller parts called atoms.

**Neuron** A body cell that passes signals to the brain about how the body feels.

**Particle** A very tiny piece of something.

**Phonograph** A machine invented in 1877 for recording and playing sound.

**Photon** A tiny light particle.

**Prosthetic** A replacement body part, such as a wooden leg.

**Quantum physics** The science of studying how very tiny pieces of matter and energy work.

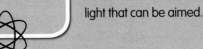

**Radioactivity** A type of energy called radiation, sent out by radioactive objects.

**Renaissance** A period roughly between the 1300s and the 1600s, when European scientists, artists and thinkers began to explore lots of new ideas.

**Scanner** A machine that detects something and uses the information to create an image.

**SOE** The Special Operations Executive, a British government department which organised spying and guerrilla fighting during World War Two.

**Spinning Jenny** A machine invented in 1769 for spinning cotton. Before this, spinning was done by hand.

**Steam engine** An engine driven by steam, created by burning coal to heat up water in a boiler.

**Stone Age** The period of time when humans only used stone tools, and did not know how to use metal.

**Teleportation** Breaking an object into tiny particles, moving them from one location to another, and reforming the particles to make the object again.

**Telescope** A machine fitted with powerful optical lenses to magnify things.

**Trephining** (also called trepanning) Cutting a hole in someone's skull, the earliest surgical operation known.

**Vacuum** A space with no air in it.

**Wormhole** A tunnel-shape in space that might connect two distant locations, or even times. Nobody knows if wormholes really exist.

# INVENTIONS WEBSITES

www.inventnow.org
Submit your own inventions and see lots of invention ideas created by kids around the world.

www.inventivekids.com
Invention fun and games to play.

www.sciencemuseum.org.uk
Lots of information and images of inventions, from the world-renowned Science Museum in London.

www.si.edu/Museums/air-and-space-museum
The online entrance to the Air and Space Museum in Washington DC, USA, full of flying machines of all kinds.

http://www.spymuseum.org/games
Play some fun spy games.

http://www.uspto.gov/web/offices/ac/ahrpa/opa/kids/
The kids' page of the United States Patent and Trademark office. Play games and find out about inventions.

## Note to parents and teachers